To Find a Stone

a first poetry collection by

Sherry Paige

Finishing Line Press
Georgetown, Kentucky

To Find a Stone

Copyright © 2018 by Sherry Paige
ISBN 978-1-63534-806-4 First Edition
All rights reserved under International and Pan-American Copyright Conventions. No part of this book may be reproduced in any manner whatsoever without written permission from the publisher, except in the case of brief quotations embodied in critical articles and reviews.

ACKNOWLEDGMENTS

Grateful acknowledgement is made to the editor of the following publication in which two of these poems previously appeared.

Hills & Hamlets: 'Birdbook,' 'The Smell of Leather'

Thanks also to my family, friends, teachers, and fellow writers who have provided wise feedback, insight and encouragement along this path; especially, Victoria Clausi, Jeff Hardin, Tiana Clark, Sandy Coomer, Karen Fentress, Anne Doolittle, Ed Holmes, Margaret B. Ingraham, Joel & Carol Tomlin, all the Landmark Poetry Reading artist friends, the Duck River Writer's Conference at Columbia State Community College and the supportive literary community of Middle Tennessee.

Publisher: Leah Maines
Editor: Christen Kincaid
Cover Art and Design: Ed Holmes
Author Photo: Ed Holmes

Printed in the USA on acid-free paper.
Order online: www.finishinglinepress.com
also available on amazon.com

Author inquiries and mail orders:
Finishing Line Press
P. O. Box 1626
Georgetown, Kentucky 40324
U. S. A.

Table of Contents

Part I

To Find a Stone 1
Teacher, Teach Me 2
Good Grief, God 3
At MacDonalds 4
Birdbook 5
Reading Mary Oliver in the Snow 6
The Wishing Well 7
The Smell of Leather 8
Opening Hunt 9
Father's Day 10
Because 11

Part II

Gravitas 14
Strings 15
Precious Cargo 17
Ambush Hill 18
Uncomfortable 19
Easter Vigil 20
On the Leaf Covered Trails 21
Just So You Know 22
Stealing from You on Palm Sunday 23
Someday I'll Love 24
Self-Portrait as a Grand Piano Soundboard 25

*This collection is dedicated to
my amazing mother,
Beverly J. Pigg*

Part One

"Lead me to the rock that is higher than I."

Psalm 61:2
New American Standard

To Find a Stone

The statuary yard holds me hostage
    with its molded rock shapes
  bearing favorite words like
      dream, hope, live, courage.

I walk among them assessing
      the change in my pocket,
  to leave at last in search of my own,
    upon which I write…

Teacher, Teach Me

… to write…to abandon routine,
        call out convention,
        expose the impertinent
        clamor of clauses
as prepositional and subordinate vie for attention.

Grammar rules alone
        will never serve to be enough
        for holding onto the substance
        of it all now. Even the moving
moment of dialogue you still can't forget—

born from study? Or stunned surprise
        from the pen of one following
        true and living words
        spilling, even now,
into a breathing habitat;

a holding pen in patient wait
        to slip below sleep
        in the coming dark
        and write their warning
upon the heart:

That all that's taught
        and all that's learned
        must rot and fall and die
        to ever pierce the fertile earth
within and spring forth blooming.

Good Grief, God

How do you bear
to look upon it,
the awful beauty
of our loss

and how are we
to bear it
while we await
the ashes of sorrow
to ignite a living flame again?

Let the wailing winds have
their way with us.
Let their gales
gust all around us

over and under us,
in, through and
out of us
forever
in spite of us,

till our grieving grip
is loosened from the past
and love's brave battle
bows to beauty's call at last.

And since we are not
strong enough to mend
our faithless fall,
send a cool, calm breeze
sweep us to our knees,
breathe gently on us, please—

till we break like bread to thank you.

At MacDonald's

…the morning I snuck
out of your house—
the stoic, metallic tables
absent familiar faces
made still and silent
vicious voices of the night,
feeding solace to my soul
with every hungry bacon bite;

the sudden secret solitude
of stranger, writer-in-the-corner,
pouring poetic license all over
my journal page.

BirdBook

The crackled grouse
       sits on the coffee table
       robin's egg blue to match the pillows.

In my chair by the window
       birdbook in hand
       I note the arrival of the dark eyed junco.

Only days earlier
       I had him by another name
       warbler, wren, finch...

But today marks a new day
       no book alone can teach;
for I see them with awakened eye,
       know them as they truly are,
can call them by their proper names—

beautiful, graceful,
       trusting, strong,
musical, grateful
       all day long.

Reading Mary Oliver in the Snow

Watching red bird
as snow falls
I can see the word
is out
Boot tracks
on the path
may have tipped
them off
and then again
my wanderings—
less interesting to them
than theirs to me—
are likely
of little notice
but etched in white
may yet
invite their snowy
search
for seed.

The Wishing Well

I forgot about the wishing well at Shell Creek
until the image
of a bucket in your barn
took me back…
my shy palm stretched
toward that soft mouth, nibbling
its pleasure at the treat I had to share;
slobbery lips tickling my skin
as I lowered myself deep into wishing water.

The Smell of Leather

I remember
        this smell of leather
The first time a dank day
        stilled us after a long run.

Trees were high
        and bright as flags waving.
Faces glistening from the teamed
        effort of getting to this rise on the land.

Lungs filled with sweet breathing—
        a kind that only happens here.
Great hearts beneath us snorting out
        their pleasure to be so alive.

I remember…
        as turkey buzzards
Graced the blue above
        like Angel Kites
You, turning to whisper…
        'God is in this place'

And we knew we followed
        more than foxes.

Opening Hunt

A love so strange and deep

Defying all we know to speak

A pomp and circumstance from early dawn

Till braid and boot can brag that they are one.

Father's Day

Surround me with stones
    all kinds
      shapes
        sizes,
with little greens peeping out
  to answer the light,
      receiving life
the only way they know how.

Add a gurgle of water
      nearby in a thicket
      of moss and frogs,
maybe even a turtle or two,
      all happy to be still
as cool ripples move about them.

Then make the dawn
    come slowly
      ray by ray
      thru shadow
and being so close to heaven
      step through its gate.

Join me on this mercy seat
      and I will read
         to you
    my poem prayer
that brought you here.

Because

Because I had a grandfather
    who kept his promise
    I got a horse when I was twelve.
Because I had a horse and loved to ride
    I fell in with a wild group
    of wanna-be cowboys;
        but,
Because I was a good girl,
    that didn't last long.
Don't think that made me prim and proper
    just because I learned to comply.

I had my own idea about everything
    and, because
    I was such a rebel in other ways,
        my innocent face
    hid the teen-age torment I lived
    mostly because

I wanted to find out who I really was;
    I wanted to be that.
Because over time I believed there was a purpose to my life
    beyond rebellion

    Now, because that sounds so wise,
        let me set the record straight.

It is only because I met you.
Because I couldn't say no…
    the way you offered yourself.

Part Two

---

*"Take from me this heart of stone ...
give me a heart of flesh."*

Ezekiel 36:26
The New Jerusalem Bible

Gravitas

Time to write us something.
What I miss and what I don't.

      How it hurts too much to talk about.
How incredulous it is that we are here,
      though signs along the way pointed to
      a cliff ahead
if we had only dared to read.

Never mind now our lack of preparation,
      shared denial
      of impending emergency exit needed.
For how does one know when to fashion an evacuation plan,
or what it will look like
      to go too far—

      until the inevitable free fall happens,
      revealing the true weight of its gravity.

Strings

With the strength of strings
on my mind today, I
marveled at the bird feeder's nylon
tether to the tree branch
swaying with six of various breeds
and later,
two squirrels vying for seed.

Not surprising
the memory of a titmouse
caught with our kite string tangled
around its leg followed
colored by the amazing tenderness
with which you knelt
to free him.

I revisited the museum art show
presenting a huge wall mural
with one half its size
suspended below
swinging at will
on a single cord tied
to the mural above.

Later, we recreated our own
with a piece of baling twine.

The grand piano strings
brought the sting…
soundboard pins bearing
2000 pounds of pressure
per square inch…the same amount
born by the human body
under great duress.

Though we promised
"no strings attached",
with you near I'm as strong
as the ski rope pulling us
up and down the river
all day behind the boat;
with you gone I am hanging

       by hope

            too thin

               to

                    hold

                         me

Precious Cargo

Heavy canvas with weathered leather trim
        suggestive of mail carriers in earlier days.
Looks important, even empty, lying ready
        each morning for its daily carry. How
many poets will be held within its calfskin
        strapping today?

How many paperback, hardback, classic,
        contemporary will challenge the fraying
fibers of construction? How many student
        or new-on-the-scene chapbooks will
co-mingle with Kennedy, Frost, Hecht, even
        Pulitzer winners?

And what kind of balanced strength will it take
        to hold this weight of insight; all impassioned
voices in various stages of focused authenticity
        and hard won inspiration. With a new day
underway, fierce fingers at the latches undo then re-secure
        buckle to strap.

What backpack would have the nerve to come
        unhinged from such precious cargo, as it's
hoisted over the shoulder, onto the back, pressed
        into the spine of the one
who most needs to carry it?

Ambush Hill

We all have one to climb
a trek not for its
pleasure or its view
but for the chance at life
it offers to a few

who brave the bramble
and the brine to
scale the real
to touch the tops
the jagged rocks
that scheme and steal.

To finally find
which footfall steady,
sure and slow
will miss the moss
that hides the slippery
way to go.

It hurts the heart,
the mind, the soul
when led astray.
All mine to learn
when came my turn
on Ambush Hill
one day.

Uncomfortable

Let me start by expressing my discomfort
in having to admit an inability
of believing you could find a way to insert
your Holy Self into our oh-so-sophisticated lifestyle
here, now.

I find myself currently bumbling about
in feeble attempts to recount how amazing this
one phone conversation tonight; one only imagined
in dreams of finally speaking the same language
with a sister

who generally shares little but the same
birth mother and father, plus brother makes
three, and yet, tonight includes Thee.
I'm pretty sure it was you there on the line
listening in,

giving the pauses in between awkward responses
a fresh breath like you are so good at.
Makes them start up again bolder. Incredulous
that two people who've known each other at such distance
for so long could speak this way.

Most remarkable of all may be the offhanded
denouement. The 'oh let me sleep on it, talk
in the morning' lightness of being—the dead
give-a-way that I love you would surely follow
this good night to bed.

Easter Vigil

The cries have stopped.
The curtain is rent.
He gave up the ghost
the Holy one.

Mourning dove calls.
If you are the word,
each letter must
be alive, too.

Irises poise
to bloom overnight.
Thorn blossoms
bow their heads.

All await the moment when
mourning births
its fresh new morn
and the living proof is in you.

To think
how we beat
your beauty
to a pulp.

On the Leaf Covered Trails

…the smell is dank after a rain;
the rocky trails above much drier
with their water running down
to pool on the leaf covered trails.
Turkey families don't mind
getting their feet wet
as they move ever so slowly
leading with their long necks
on the leaf covered trails.
What is under the leaves, you ask?
How deep, I say?
The earthworm crawls
on the leaf covered trails
and knows them as we never will
so, should I trip and fall and die
one mid-October
think of me as happy to receive
the breeze that stirs
such blanket from the trees
gently falling round me
on the leaf covered trails.

Just So You Know

I'm not ashamed
      of the way my skin
needed yours to feel alive.

Nor, any of the moments
      I felt at home there
next to you.

In the late hours of evening
      or early morning just before dawn,
when longing arrests all soundness of sleep

and sole solitude stirs its most
      secret confession, my heart's
soul reaches out to soothe

the skin search here in these sheets;
      so honorably without you,
it mimics virtue.

Stealing from You on Palm Sunday

…seems unforgivable
as trees wave their breezy tops
like palm branches in echo
of children singing
your donkey entry to the city;
adult choir minus an alto;
this of all days, but one,
I should be there.

Yet, here at the window,
journal pressed lap down
eyes briefly raised,
I grip my palm pen
and pray this coffee
communion real enough
for you to ride through
my gates, too.

Someday I'll Love

Don't be afraid.
Breathe slowly, deeply.
Allow control of the moment to fall away.
Balance is not the issue.
Attention to the present is all there is.
Perfection will never be your truest mark.
Authenticity is the best companion
seeing you through all that is to come.

The shadow of a faith
in the flow of what's
real, alive and breathing
can carry you through much.
Love the way you've come
to see and recognize—
then keep looking as the puzzle
pieces fall into place.

This is the instrument
your fingers love to touch,
live to touch. Feel around.
Bring all that's yours into the room
together at last. For one brief moment,
not even to love each other,
but to be at peace, finally
in each other's presence.

Self-Portrait as a Grand Piano Soundboard

Two thousand pounds of pressure
per square inch is the math equation
for my tight grip on pins
wrapped in metallic string.
Stay strong and hold on
is the marching order of my every day.
A master created me to draw
those who might release the life within me.

The silent, patient one
I strive to be in tune with
what is played in any key,
holding my statuesque pose
for a lifetime if need be.

Did I mention how strong I am?
How my mannerly presence suggests
that all rooms are parlors, where I
await your gift of time

for tea, perhaps, or a story
or two shared between friends;
or a concert hall where,
even in repose, with no one

close enough to caress me, some say
they can feel the beating of my heart,
the rhythm of my breathing,
hear a tinkling of the melody
I long to leave you with
I long to leave you with
I long to leave you with

A Note from the Author

Many thanks to my publisher, Finishing Line Press, for their
consideration of this material and faithful support
to the creative writing arts—
particularly the genre of poetry.

*"Write, therefore, what you
have seen."*

Revelation 1:19
King James Version

Born and raised in Columbia, (Maury County), Tennessee, **Sherry Paige** graduated from Vanderbilt University. Her multi-faceted career has spanned the creative arts as a composer, writer, and producer of music, film/video, and theater. Her musical theater composition, No Small Miracle, was the runner-up to the first Michael Stewart Award; his Broadway musical, 42 Street, well known as a classic today.

Following the loss of her home, its contents, and beloved baby grand piano, Paige set out to rebuild her life from the devastating Nashville Flood of 2010. Some three years later, having put her music back together, she recorded a solo piano album known simply as The Piano Project.

Currently living in Nashville, Tennessee, she continues her artistic passions and is honored to offer her first collection of poetry, *To find a stone*.

To find a stone by Sherry Paige offers a fresh poetic voice crafting beautifully created lines filled with intimacy and depth, leading the reader through all the senses with a wonderful balance of tension and abandonment. An absolutely wonderful first volume!

Tricia Walker—award-winning songwriter; two-time nominee, Mississippi Institute of Arts & Letters; Board of Governors—The Recording Academy, Memphis Chapter.

www.ingramcontent.com/pod-product-compliance
Lightning Source LLC
LaVergne TN
LVHW041514070426
835507LV00012B/1562